Jazz Guitar Improvisation

by Sid Jacobs

PLAYBACK+
Speed • Pitch • Balance • Loop

To access audio and video visit:
www.halleonard.com/mylibrary
Enter Code
2100-5088-4677-5272

Audio accompaniment by Ron Berman

Cover guitar courtesy of Crown Music Milwaukee, Wisconsin

ISBN 978-1-4950-8880-3

7777 W. BLUEMOUND RD. P.O. BOX 13819 MILWAUKEE, WI 53213

Visit Hal Leonard Online at
www.halleonard.com

Contents

ABOUT THE AUTHOR

Sid Jacobs was born in Miami, Florida and began taking guitar lessons at the age of seven. As a teenager he became serious about playing jazz and would practice by day and sneak into jazz clubs at night. When the Jacobs family moved to Nevada, he obtained a position as guitar instructor at the University of Nevada, Las Vegas. This made him, at eighteen, the youngest faculty member in the school's music department. While living in Nevada, Sid found work in hotel pit orchestras and as a touring accompanist for various popular singers and jazz artists.

After moving to Los Angeles, he organized curriculum for the Jazz Guitar elective at the Musicians Institute (GIT) and the Advanced Bebop and Jazz Guitar elective at the Dick Grove School. His CD, *It's Not Goodnight*--a straight-ahead blowing session featuring his original compositions--was released in 1991. Sid has been featured in performance with Eddie Harris, Harold Land, Buddy Montgomery, and Joe Diorio.

Through his involvement in education and his associations with jazz artists, Sid Continues to gain recognition as an educator and performing artist. In a live performance review, Los Angeles Times jazz critic Don Heckman characterized him as "...a highly articulate improviser...never at a loss for a new phrase, his improvisations seemed to unfold with the ever-changing fascination of a set of Bach variations."

Sid currently divides his time among his pursuits as GIT instructor, product consultant, clinician and performing artist.

Sid Jacobs uses Thomastic-Infeld strings and plays a Borys guitar.

INTRODUCTION ▶

The purpose of this book is to acquaint the guitarist with some of the tools and vocabulary used in jazz improvizing, with an emphasis on the bebop and post-bebop styles. As with any language, the more vocabulary you have, the better prepared you are to express yourself.

It's taken all my life to learn what not to play.
—Dizzy Gillespie

Music needs contrast to be interesting. The concepts of dynamics and use of space are readily understood by the intellect, yet rarely are they effectively applied. Whenever you are listening or playing, observe the lengths of the phrases, the articulation, the accents, and the spaces between phrases. Become more aware of your breathing and sing your phrases as you play them, even if only the rhythm and articulation. Inspiration, the mind and the heart, are directly connected to the breath— to inspire literally means to "to breathe into." Pauses between breaths occur naturally in conversation. This allows the idea conveyed to be acknowledged. The same holds true in ensemble improvising, where the use of space also allows for interplay among the musicians. All of the great masters of jazz improvisation have made artful use of space.

Begin to build a repertoire of standards and jazz tunes. There are literally thousands to choose from, and the ones you choose to learn and commit to memory reflect who you are as an artist. Spend time just listening to music, particularly the music you wish to play. Total immersion is the most effective way to learn any language. Transcribing solos is also highly recommended. Choose highlights from your favorite solos and learn to play them accurately. This will develop both your ear and your technique. The music you listen to is the nourishment of your musical life, and like the food you eat, will come out with or without your blessing. You are what you eat, what you listen to, and the sum total of your life experiences.

The musical path is not so much a matter of sharpening the tools as it is awakening the creative mind. We are dealing with the creative process and not merely a set of licks, techniques, and exercises. There is no formula for art.

Music is your own experience, your thoughts,
your wisdom. If you don't live it, it won't come out
of your horn.
—Charlie Parker

CHAPTER 1

DIATONIC SCALE REVIEW

Let's begin by reviewing the diatonic scales: the major, the harmonic minor, the melodic minor, and their corresponding modes or chord scales. Since jazz playing involves improvising over a chord progression ("blowing over changes"), it is essential to know the chord tones and chord scales.

Fig. 1 - C Major Scale

	C	D	E	F	G	A	B
I⁷(Cmaj7)	Root	9th	3rd	(11th/4th)	5th	6th	maj7th
ii⁷(Dm7)	♭7th	Root	9th	♭3rd (minor 3rd)	11th	5th	6th/13th
V⁷(G7)	(11th)	5th	13th	♭7th	Root	9th	3rd
IV⁷(Fmaj7)	5th	6th	maj7th	Root	9th	3rd	♯11th/♭5th

Columns show the function of the above note within the chord at left. For example: column 1, row 2 illustrates the note "C" as the "♭7th" of Dm7.

◯ = Avoid Notes

Fig. 2 - Major Scale Modes

Major scale starting on:

First Degree	Ionian Mode
Second Degree	Dorian Mode
Third Degree	Phrygian Mode
Fourth Degree	Lydian Mode
Fifth Degree	Mixolydian Mode
Sixth Degree	Aeolian Mode
Seventh Degree	Locrian Mode

C MAJOR SCALE FINGERINGS

The following three-octave symmetrical fingerings will help you visualize the neck. You may be surprised how easily these scale fingerings transpose to all keys. The first fingering starts on the fifth degree of the scale with a position shift. Each time we arrive at the fifth degree of the scale, we repeat the same fingering pattern.

Fig. 3

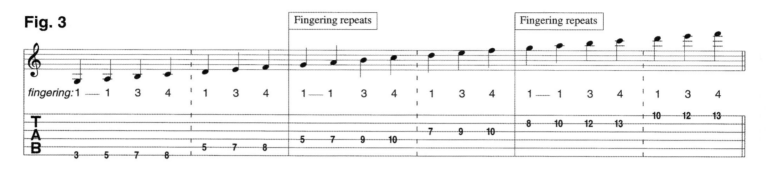

Notice the repeating pattern: 1–1–3–4/1–3–4.

This next fingering starts on the sixth degree of the scale (A). There is a position shift between the sixth and seventh degrees (A and B). This fingering is identical in each octave.

Fig. 4

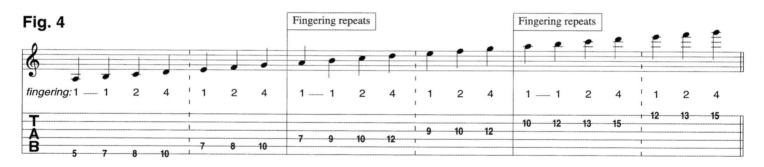

Notice the repeating pattern: 1–1–2–4/1–2–4.

Fig. 5 - A Harmonic Minor Scale

	A	B	C	D	E	F	G#
I (Am)	Root	2nd/9th	♭3rd (minor 3rd)	4th/11th	5th	♭6th	maj7th
ii∅7 (Bm7♭5)	♭7th	Root	♭2nd/♭9th	♭3rd	4th/11th	♭5th	6th
V7 (E7)	4th/11th	5th	♭13th/♯5th	♭7th	Root	♭9th	3rd

◯ = avoid notes

In using scales to improvise over chord changes, we sometimes encounter *avoid notes.* An experienced improviser will naturally avoid conflicting notes or artfully deal with them. To avoid doesn't necessarily mean to not play at all, but to play with discretion and direction.

HARMONIC MINOR FINGERINGS ▶

The following fingerings are based on the C major fingerings you just learned. The only difference between the C major scale and the A harmonic minor scale is the G♯ found in the A harmonic minor scale.

The first fingering starts on the seventh degree (G♯) of the A harmonic minor scale. Compare this with the major scale fingering that starts on the fifth degree; both fingerings repeat the pattern: 1–1–3–4/1–3–4.

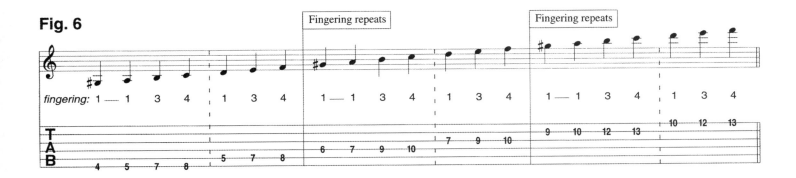

This next fingering for A harmonic minor is based on the second C major scale fingering. Both fingerings repeat the pattern: 1–1–2–4/1–2–4.

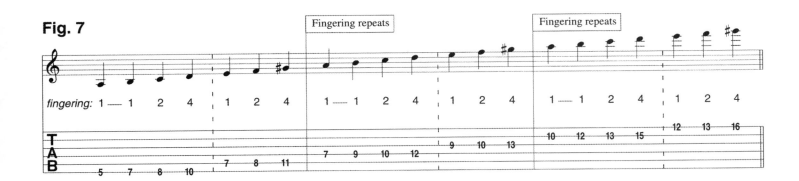

Fig. 8 - C Melodic Minor Scale

	C	D	♭E	F	G	A	B
i⁷(Cm7) melodic minor	Root	9th	♭3rd	11th	5th	6th	maj7th
IV⁷(F7) Lydian ♭7	5th	13th	♭7th	Root	9th	3rd	♯11th
vii B7 altered B7 Altered	♭9th	♯9th	3rd D♯	♯11th/♭5th	♭13th/♯5th	♭7th	Root
viø7 (Am7♭5) Locrian ♯2	♭3rd	11th	♭5th	♭6th	♭7th	Root	9th

MELODIC MINOR FINGERINGS ▶

These fingerings for the melodic minor scale are based on the previous fingerings for the major scale. The difference between C major and C melodic minor is that in C melodic minor, the E natural becomes E♭.

The first fingering starts on the fifth degree of the scale. In this scale, the fingering pattern becomes: 1–1–3–4/1–2–4.

Fig. 9

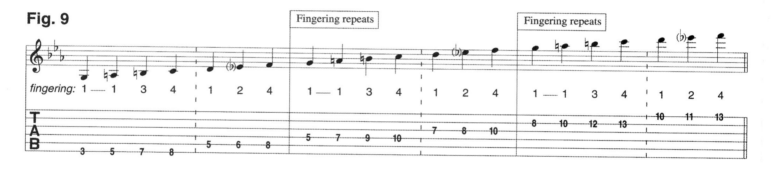

This fingering starts on the sixth degree of the melodic minor scale. The repeated fingering pattern becomes 1–1–2–4/1–3–4.

Fig. 10

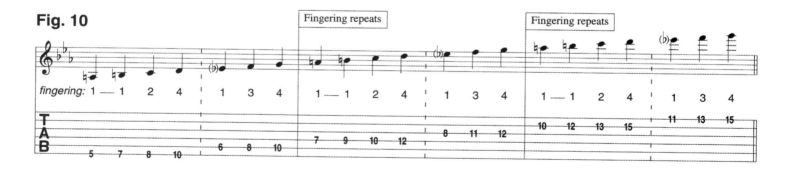

Theoretically, the starting note of a scale determines the mode. However, in real playing situations, the harmonic environment created by the bass or chordal instrument actually starts the scale. Therefore, you are free to begin your melodic idea (or scale) on whichever note you choose. Factors to consider might be rhythmic placement or continuing the previous phrase. One phrase should naturally follow another. You should be able to connect your chord scales at the closest available note.

Jazz improvising has been described as a combination of athletics and aesthetics. A musician who improvises must be fluent and articulate.

CHAPTER 2
APPLYING SCALES AND ARPEGGIOS

Nothing outlines harmony more clearly than chord tones. We must know how to "spell" any chord and know several different fingerings. Obviously there is more than one place on the guitar to play the same phrase. To be a proficient improviser we must be able to name and play the chord tones, extensions, and alterations of any given chord. One must be able to start an idea from any note in the chord (or chord scale), in any position.

Sometimes we learn a melodic idea and it might start on the ninth of the chord or the eleventh or thirteenth and so on. When we improvise over a chord progression, we need to know where the chord tones are and be able to access this information instantaneously. It takes time for this to occur, but ultimately it becomes intuitive.

For example, by now we all know a few movable shapes of a minor seventh chord, which we can play automatically. Similarly, we may have a few melodic fragments under our fingers that suggest a given chord. We combine these fragments to make longer phrases.

The next example is a common jazz phrase, and several fingerings are offered. If you play this phrase over a Dm7 chord, it starts on the ninth. If you play this phrase over G13, it starts on the thirteenth. Two fingerings (from the starting note E) are given from the first string, two fingerings on the second string, and two fingerings on the third string.

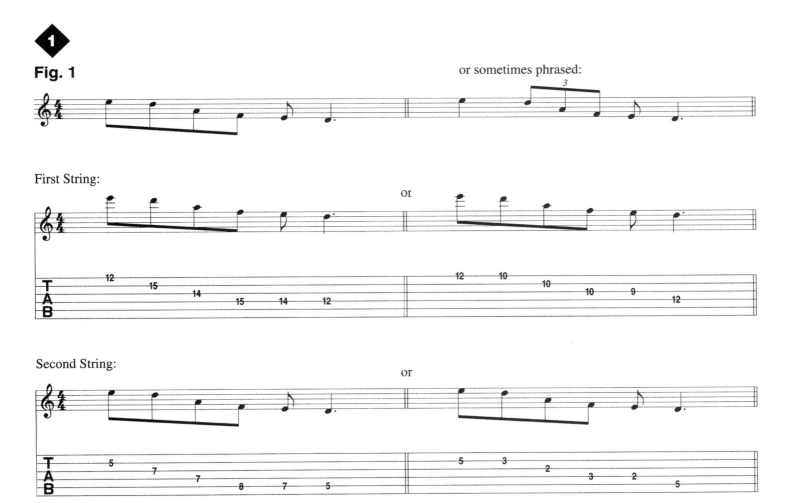

Fig. 1

First String:

Second String:

Third String:

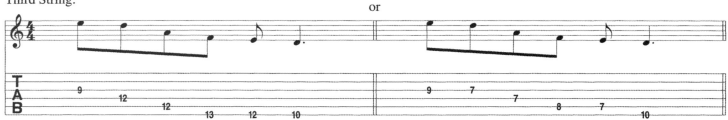

Running changes refers to arpeggiating the chord you are improvising on.

2 ◆ **Fig. 2**

We can play arpeggios based on triads or seventh chords which are part of the upper voices (chord tones).

3 ◆ **Fig. 3**

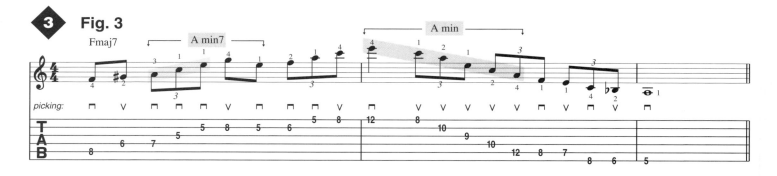

This line works over C major or Am7. C–E–G–B=Cmaj7; A–(C–E–G–B)=Am9.

4 ◆ **Fig. 4**

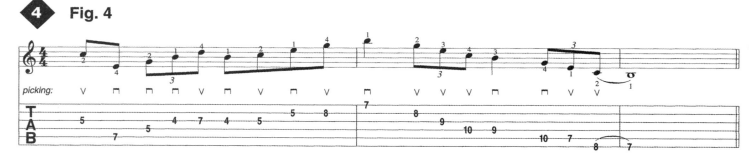

We can construct scalar runs that will align chord tones with stressed beats…

5 ◆ **Fig. 5**

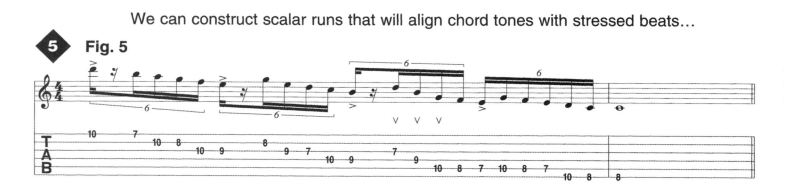

...or use a scale run to "target" a melody note.

Fig. 6

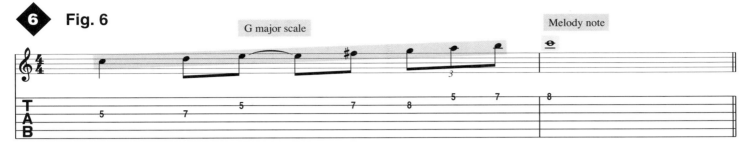

G major scale

Melody note

While the notes G–B–D–F–A–E spell out a G13 chord, often an Fmaj7♭5 arpeggio can be used to imply the harmony. After all, if we put an Fmaj7♭5 chord over a "G" in the bass, we have a G13 chord.

Fig. 7A

Fmaj7♭5

G13:	G	F	A	B	E
	Root	♭7th	9th	3rd	13th

Fig. 7B

Fig. 7C

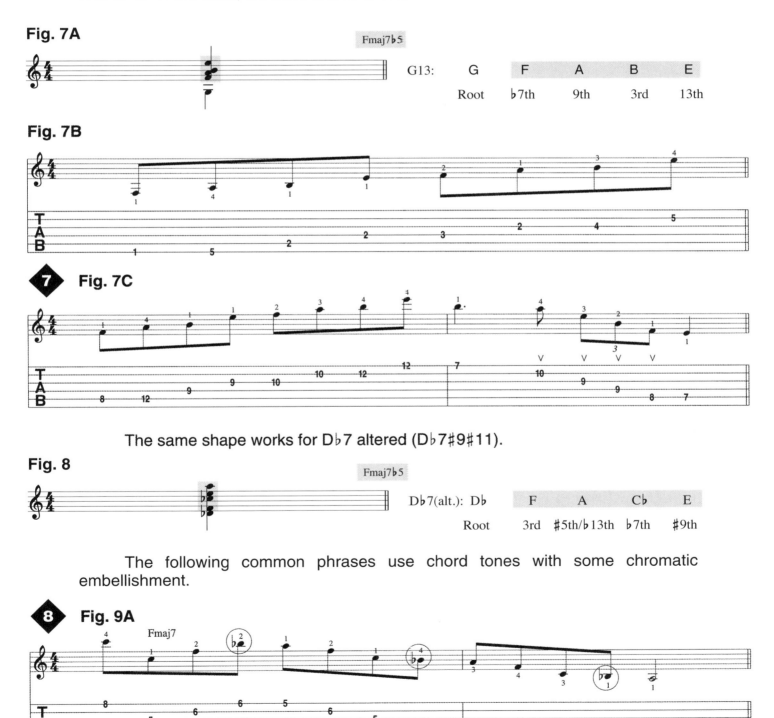

The same shape works for D♭7 altered (D♭7♯9♯11).

Fig. 8

Fmaj7♭5

D♭7(alt.):	D♭	F	A	C♭	E
	Root	3rd	♯5th/♭13th	♭7th	♯9th

The following common phrases use chord tones with some chromatic embellishment.

Fig. 9A

Fmaj7

○ = Chromatic embellishment tones

Fig. 9B - Further embellishments on 9A

○ = chromatic embellishment tones

Fig. 9C

○ = chromatic embellishment tones

This phrase combines shapes outlining a G triad and an A♭ triad, and can be used in a common I–vi–ii–V–I progression.

9 **Fig. 10**

Combining triads opens many other possibilities. Two simple major triads and their inversions can create interesting lines. This line combines A♭ major and D major triads and their inversions. Try it over A♭7(♭9♭5) or D7(♭9♭5).

10 **Fig. 11**

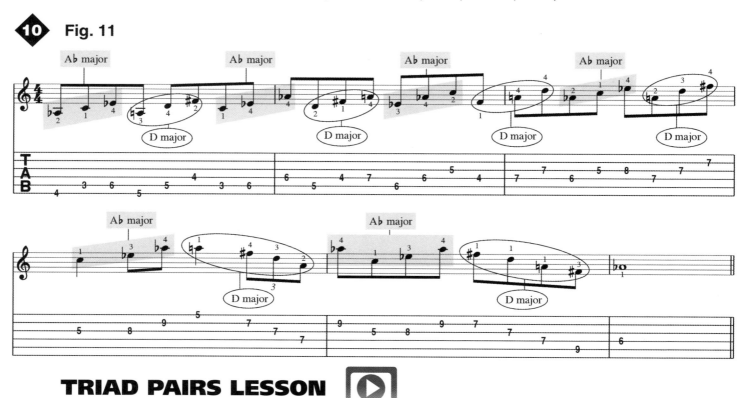

TRIAD PAIRS LESSON ▶️

CHAPTER 3
DEVELOPING A SOLO

The tools an improviser uses are the same tools used by a composer. Music can be broadly defined as "organized sound" and we use the tools to do this. Along with scales and chord tones which outline the harmony, improvisers use motifs and sequences as melodic devices in developing a solo. The Harvard Dictionary of Music defines a motif as "...a short figure of characteristic design that recurs throughout a piece of music..." It acts as a unifying element. As few as two notes may form a motif if their melody or rhythm is distinctive. A sequence can be defined simply as "a repetition of a short musical phrase at another pitch." Compositionally, the sequence acts as an element of logical continuation.

In the following excerpt (from an old Russian folk song) we see a simple motif (scale step–scale step–fourth) starting on the sixth degree of the G major scale. In the third measure, we see it repeated (sequenced) down a scale step, this time starting on the fifth degree of the scale. In the fifth measure, we see the same phrase diatonically sequenced down another scale step. In measure seven it is sequenced again, this time altered to fit the transition to relative minor.

11   Fig. 1

In this simple piece, a short phrase is repeated throughout the form. This illustrates the concept of motif repetition as a unifying element—a common practice in blues tunes.

12 UNIT Y

by Sid Jacobs

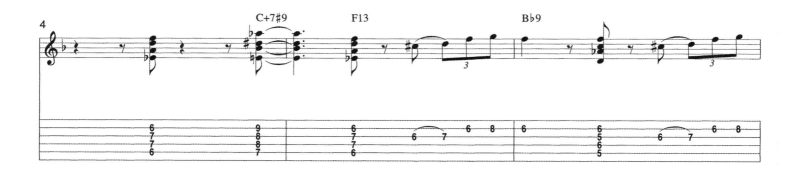

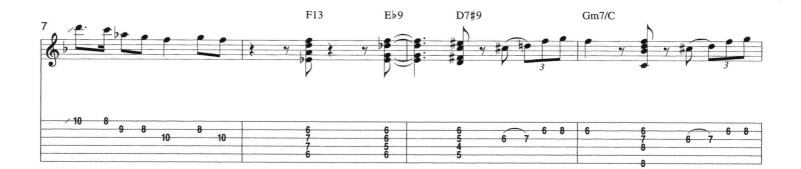

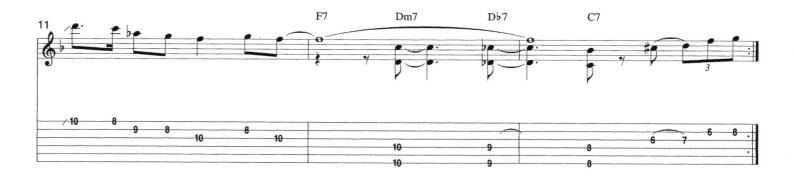

In this piece the opening phrase is repeated. It is altered slightly with each repetition to imply the harmony occurring at the time.

◆13 CHRONIC FREQUENCY
by Sid Jacobs

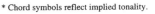
w/ pick & fingers

* Chord symbols reflect implied tonality.

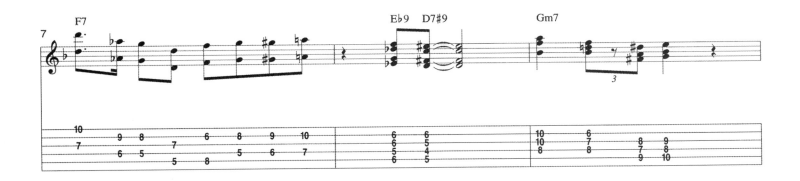

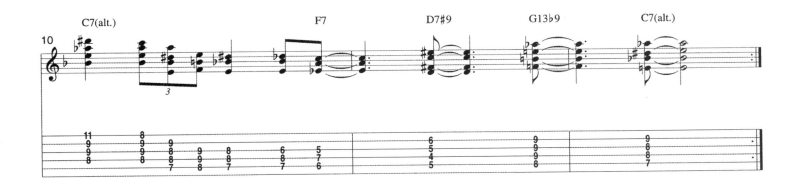

The next etude, "Consequentially," uses a sequence as a means of logical continuation. The phrase in measure 1 is repeated *without alteration* down a whole step (a *real* sequence) in measure 2, and down another step in measure 3, followed by a new phrase in measure 4. Measures 5–8 are a repetition of the first four measures down a half step. In the first two measures of letter A, a new phrase is introduced and repeated with a slight alteration in the next two measures. Then the phrase is repeated up a fourth. The phrase in measure 18 echoes the phrase in measure 17 by sequencing down a step and following the blues progression. This melodic device is used extensively by improvisers, songwriters, and composers.

◆14 CONSEQUENTIALLY

by Sid Jacobs

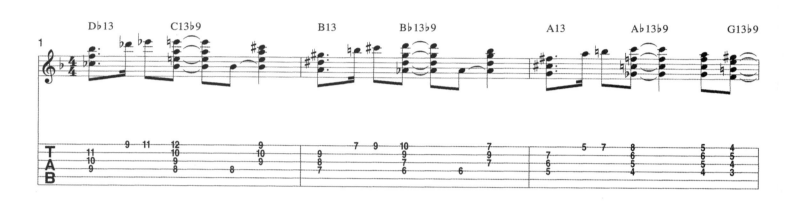

* Chord symbols reflect implied tonality.

A FEW WORDS ABOUT "FEEL"

Swinging is a natural phenomenon in music and has never been satisfactorily explained by formula. The dotted eighth and sixteenth or the triplet feel don't adequately convey the concept. While walking, your arms move in a reverse rhythm to your legs, and an attempt to *force a change or maintain a constancy* in this natural and always subtly changing counter-rhythm results in a stiffer and more labored step.

Jazz has always been music of artful syncopation. The use of a three pulse against two pulse helps to create rhythmic tension and is often used in contemporary music.

Balance is always changing

A typical four-measure phrase in common time (4/4) has thirty-two eighth notes. If we break this up into groups of three, we get ten groups of three and one group of two. A simple way of looking at it might be eight groups of three eighth notes (24) and one measure of 4/4 (8).

Fig. 2

Practice the next two phrases to get the feeling of playing across the barline.

15 **Fig. 3**

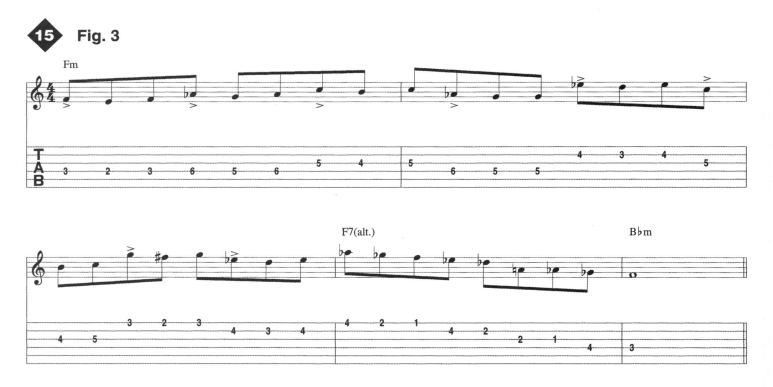

16 **Fig. 4**

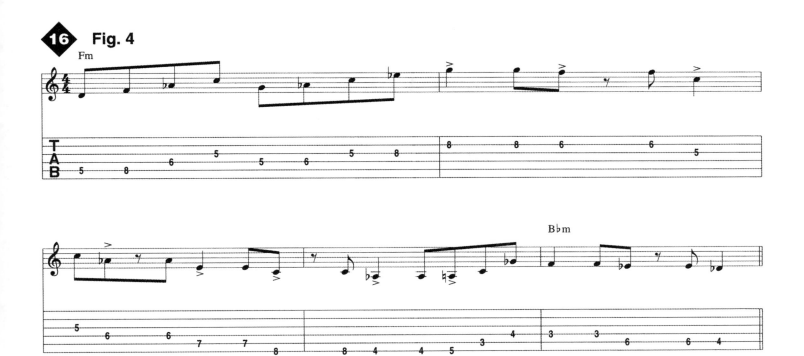

CHAPTER 4

COMMON PHRASES

In this unit we will focus on some of the phrases common to the jazz language. As previously mentioned, it is important to know the chord tones, extensions and alterations of the harmony you are dealing with. For example, some of the phrases you choose to put into your vocabulary might start on the ninth of the minor seventh chord or the sharp-ninth of the dominant seventh chord. Often you will connect the smaller phrases together to make longer lines.

A suggestion for practice might be to take some of these lines made from connected phrase fragments and work them through the cycle of fifths and the chord changes of a jazz or standard tune.

A COMMON PHRASE REVISITED

The first phrase we will look at is one of the more commonly heard phrases in the jazz lexicon. Other fingering possibilities were covered in Chapter 2.

This common phrase is often played over Dm7 and starts on the ninth of the chord. Another way to look at this phrase is as a G13 with the phrase beginning on the thirteenth. Most of the vocabulary we use over a Dm7 chord is interchangeable with a G7 chord that isn't altered. (It is common to precede a V7 chord with the iim7 chord.) In sections where the harmony stays on the dominant chord (static harmony) you will often hear a ii-V7 occuring to maintain interest in the accompaniment. Many of the lines you might play for Dm7 will work for G7 as well as Bm7♭5 as they come from the same tonal center.

If this same phrase were played over a Bm7♭5, it would start on the eleventh. For D♭7(alt.), the phrase would start on the sharp-nine.

Fig. 1

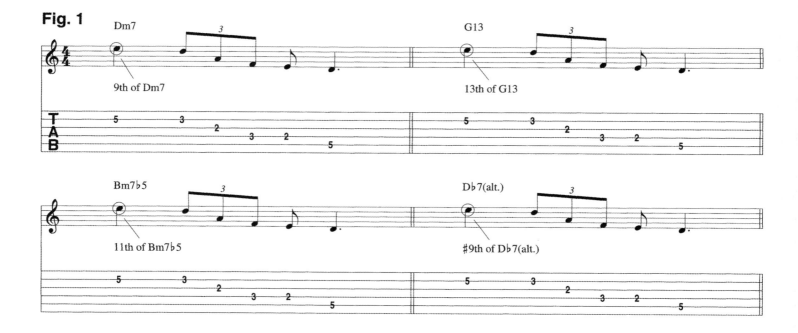

Here is the same phrase used in context of a ii–V–I progression.

Fig. 2A

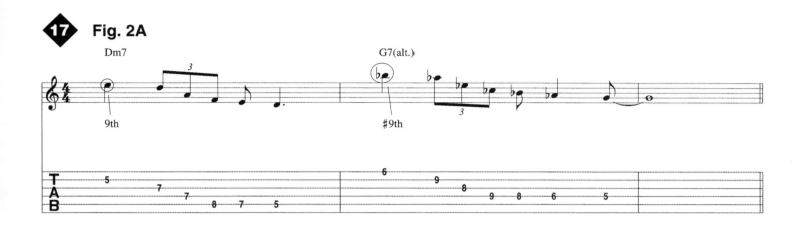

Here is another idea using the same phrase.

Fig. 2B

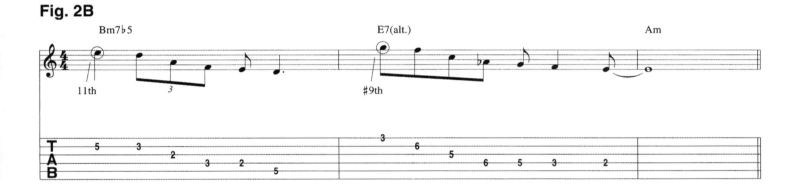

Fig. 3

GUIDE TONES

These "guide tones" (the flatted-seventh note of ii7 to the third of V7) are useful in suggesting the motion of this harmony.

Fig. 4

The sound of these notes in the context of the C major tonality suggest a ii–V sound. We can see the flatted-seventh of ii resolving to the third of V, or sus4–3 in relation to V. These are common phrase fragments that suggest the motion of Dm7–G7.

Fig. 5

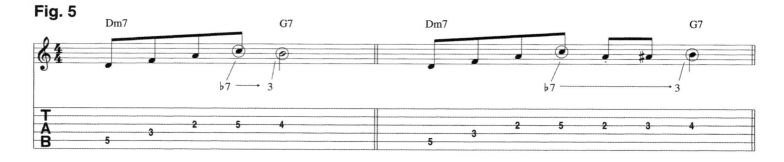

Here is a turnaround that highlights the above guide tones (the flatted-seventh of ii to the third of V7) and the third of V to the flatted-ninth of V.

19 **Fig. 6**

This example is in the style of Charlie Parker.

20 **Fig. 7**

Here is another common phrase fragment that works for Dm7, G7, and Bm7♭5.

Fig. 8

Here is the previous phrase used in the context of a ii–V–I progression.

21 Fig. 9A

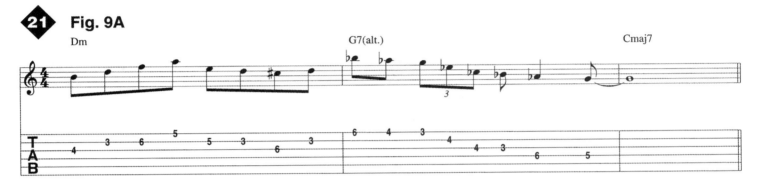

Fig. 9B

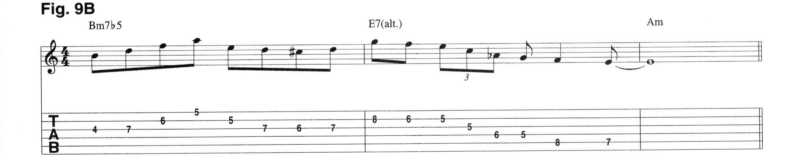

This is another phrase in Charlie Parker's style.

22 Fig. 10

CHROMATICALLY DESCENDING LINES

This descending chromatic line is common in chordal phrases and is woven into melodic phrases.

Fig. 11

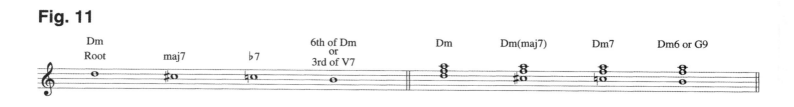

Here it is in several common phrases.

23 **Fig. 12**

This solo excerpt is one of many examples where this motion is suggested.

24 **Fig. 13**

And here is an excerpt in the style of John Coltrane.

25 **Fig. 14**

Another phrase fragment we see quite often in jazz solos is this characteristic chromatic (descent) from the fourth degree to the minor third degree of a ii chord, or from the root to the flatted-seventh degree of a dominant chord.

Fig. 15

It is very commonly heard, as in these phrases…

◀ ▶ **Fig. 16**

…and combined with the previously discussed line cliché…

◀ ▶ **Fig. 17**

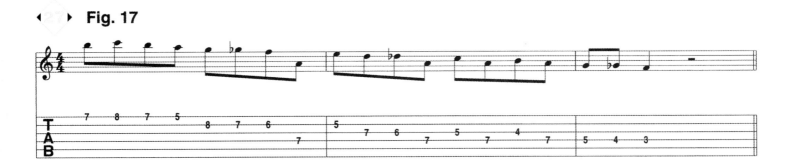

We see things like this often in John Coltrane's music.

◀ ▶ **Fig. 18**

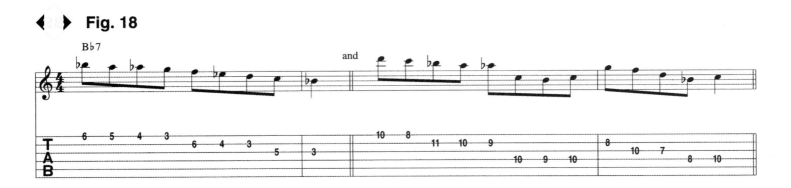

This line combines the two phrases previously discussed.

Here are some more variations with chords and double stops.

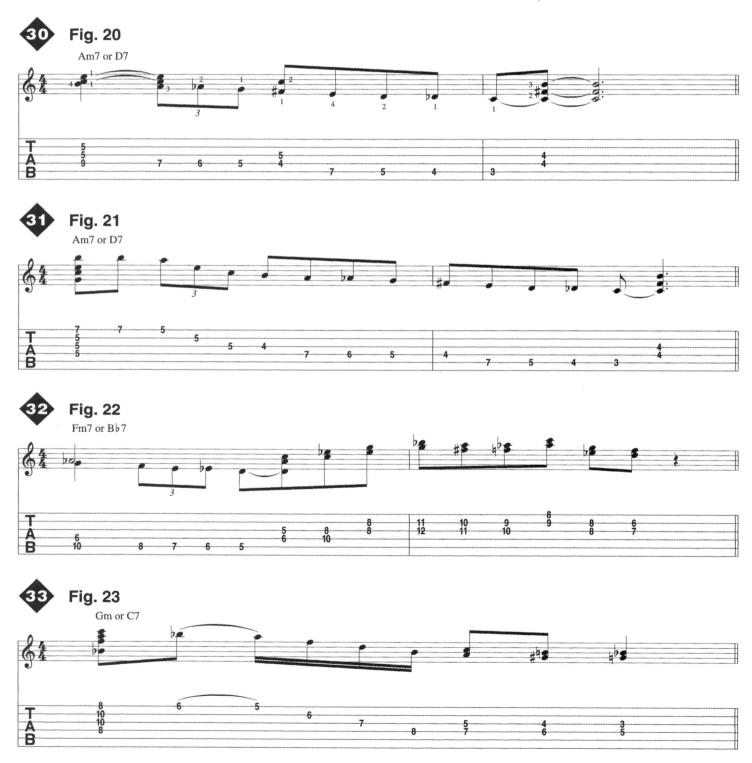

PHRASING IN A ii-V ENVIRONMENT

Here are a couple long lines with connected phrase fragments common to a ii–V harmonic environment. Try starting these lines at different spots for a shorter phrase.

◀ ▶ **Fig. 24**

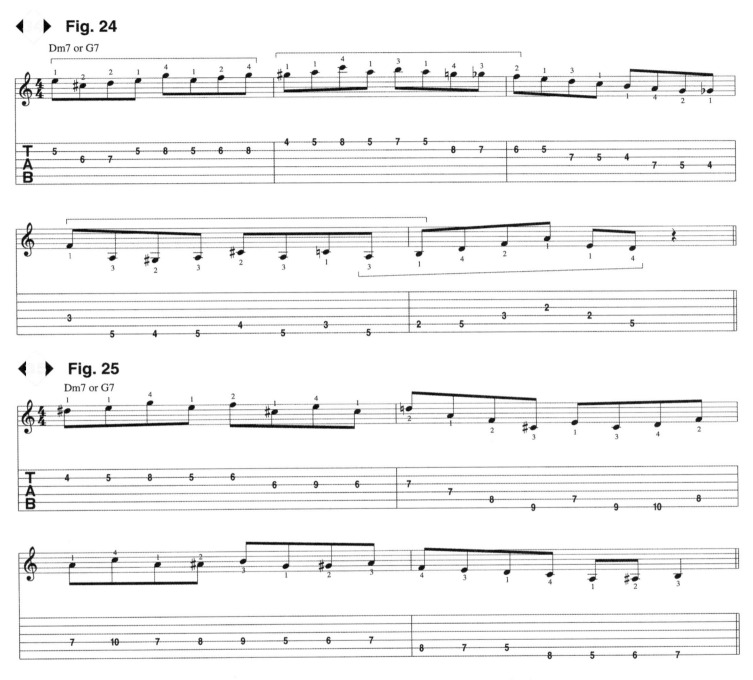

Here are some triplet phrases connected with sweep picking.

◀ ▶ **Fig. 26**

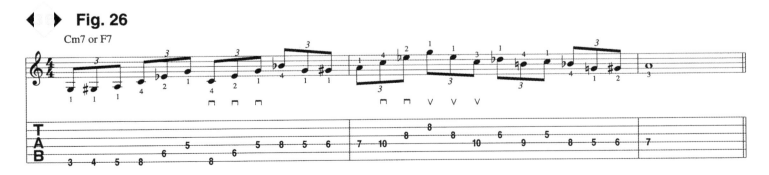

CHAPTER 5
COMMON PHRASE RESOLUTIONS

Much of jazz and popular music relies heavily on the standard ii–V7–I progression, and many compositions go through several keys using this formula. The advanced improviser can play a single-note solo through a series of modulations and you will hear the changes. Having a vocabulary of phrases that suggest the V7–I resolution will facilitate this process.

In this chapter we will focus on jazz lines that suggest the V7–I resolution. Much of the vocabulary we play on the ii7 chord is interchangeable with the vocabulary we would play on the corresponding V7 chord in the same key; but at the point of resolution, the harmony often becomes more altered, giving definition to the transition.

Let's start by going back to our familiar common phrase:

Fig. 1

This idea has several applications—it should be learned single-note style, as well as in octaves and chords.

37 Fig. 2 - Octaves

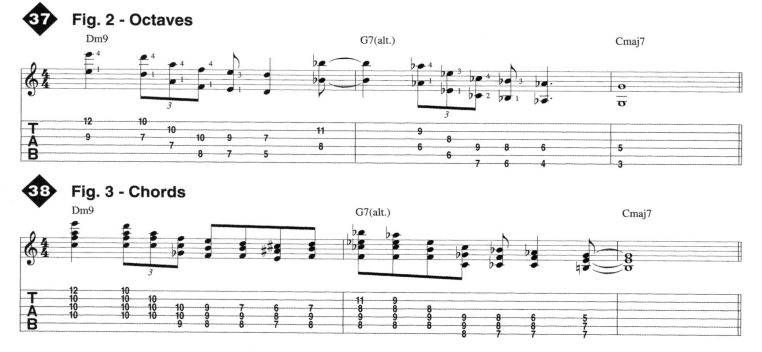

38 Fig. 3 - Chords

This example mixes chords and single notes to play the same line.

39 Fig. 4

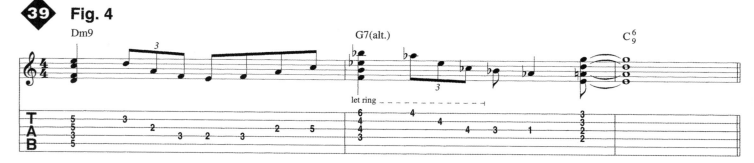

These phrase fragments highlight the motion of the third to the flatted-ninth of the dominant chord.

Fig. 5A

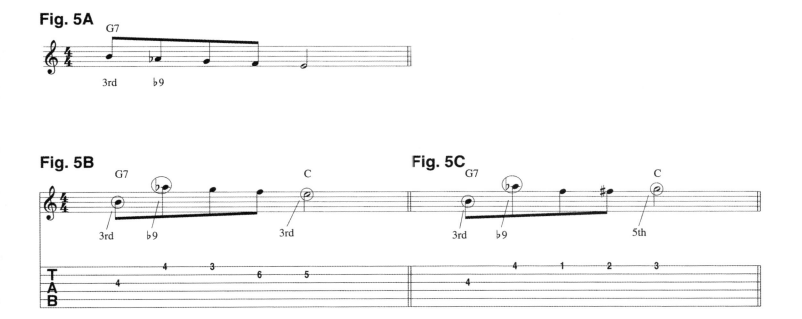

Fig. 5B   **Fig. 5C**

This example is similar to something Charlie Parker might play.

40 Fig. 6

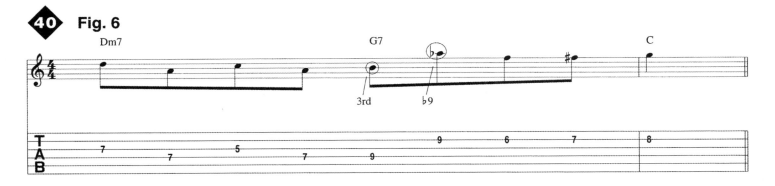

Here is a turnaround from the "Bird lick" library.

41 Fig. 7

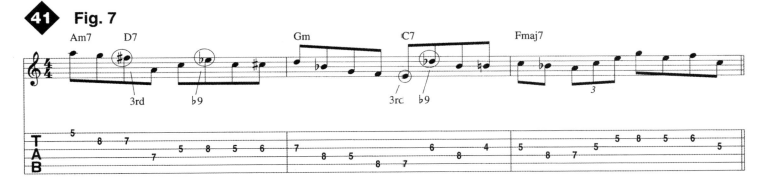

Notice the similar resolutions in the above two examples. Figure 6 in Chapter 4 is another good example of third to flat-nine motion.

USE OF THE ALTERED SCALE

Here we use the altered scale to resolve to the third of a major chord.

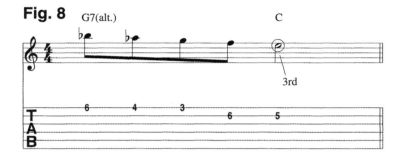

Now we use the altered scale to resolve to the fifth.

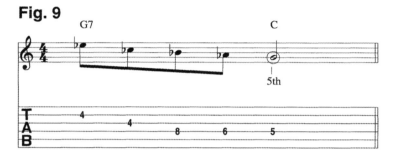

Combining the two above fragments is also a handy eight-note phrase (eight eighth notes makes one measure of 4/4).

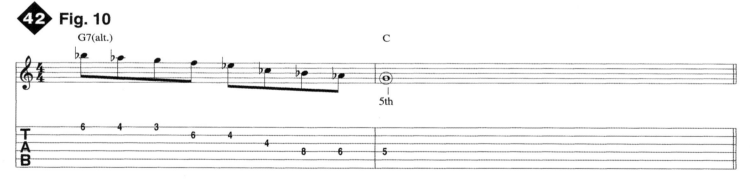

As with all the vocabulary, try this line in all keys. Here it is in octaves.

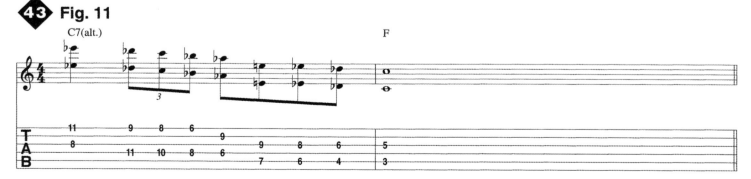

Here's the same line in thirds.

44 **Fig. 12**

Now try it with chords.

45 **Fig. 13**

The following triplet lines are based on the altered scale.

46 **Fig. 14**

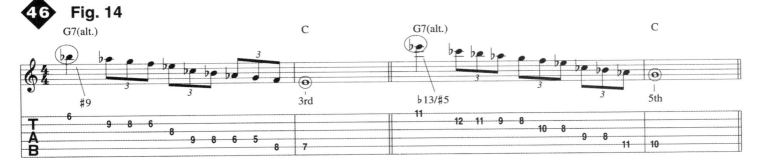

This line implies the tritone substitution of V–I, which is ♭II–I.

47 **Fig. 15**

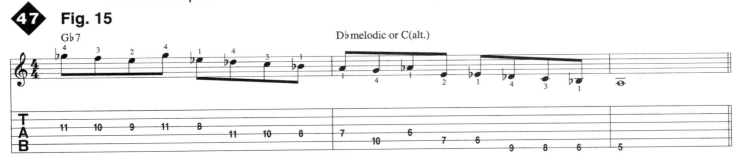

This phrase includes some sweeps and triplets.

48 **Fig. 16**

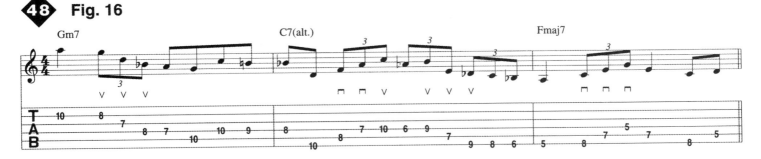

CHAPTER 6
COMMON MAJOR PHRASES

In this chapter we will focus on some of the common phrases that suggest a major sound. A major 7 chord is often interchangeable with a major 6 chord or a major 6/9 chord.

This line has the fourth resolving to the third in a major setting.

Fig. 1

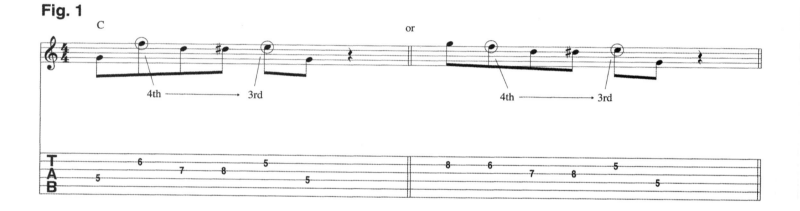

These excerpts are both in the style of Charlie Parker.

49 Fig. 2

RUNNING CHANGES

It is not unusual to see parts of solos where the improviser *spells out* the chords (running changes). It is useful to have your ideas in a rhythmic unit that is accessible.

Fig. 3

Begin to practice your lines in a rhythmic context, like one-measure or two-measure phrases—just as if you were comping chords. This example goes through the cycle of fifths.

50 **Fig. 4**

These melodic fragments outline a major sixth chord.

Fig. 5

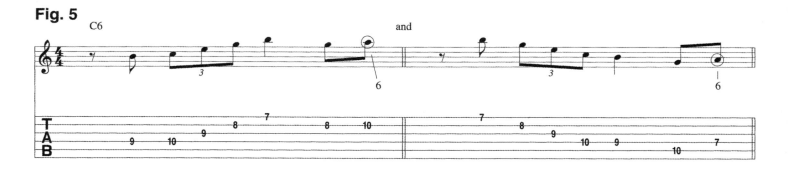

These outline a major 6/9 chord.

Fig. 6

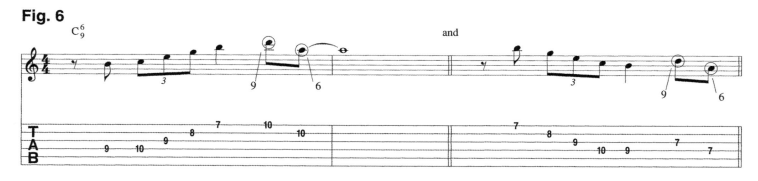

You might practice these lines in a rhythmic context up and down the neck to get a feel for playing them in an actual performance.

51 Fig. 7

34

This example is based on a common Charlie Parker phrase.

52 **Fig. 8**

Here's another maj7 "Bird-type" lick.

53 **Fig. 9**

Yet another Bird cliché:

54 **Fig. 10**

CHROMATIC MOTION BETWEEN CHORD TONES

The following examples are some common lines highlighting chromatic motion between the fifth and sixth degree of the major chord.

Fig. 11

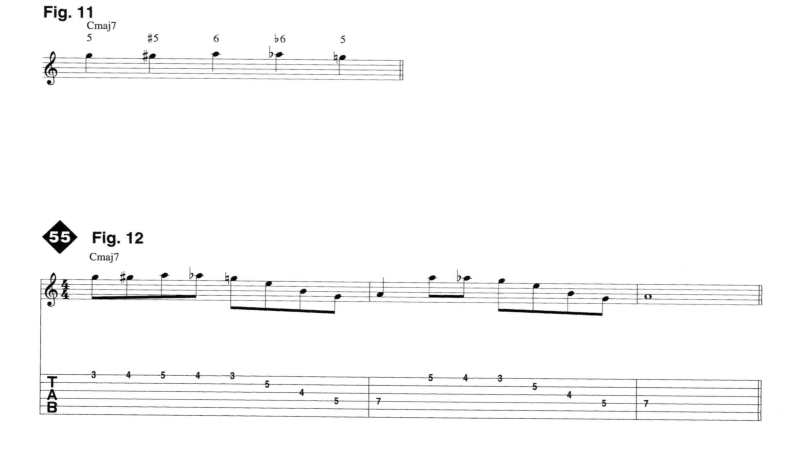

55 Fig. 12

56 Fig. 13

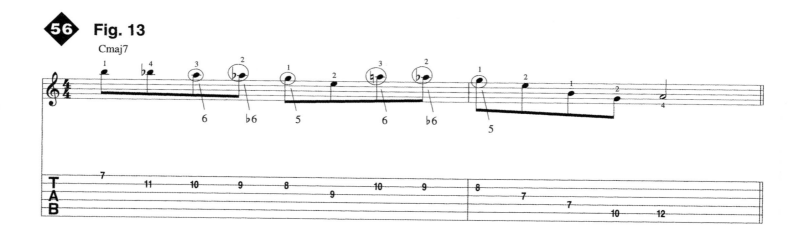

These lines combine a couple of the previously discussed fragments.

57 **Fig. 14**

This line is a Charlie Parker-type phrase.

59 **Fig. 16**

Here's another line in the style of Bird.

60 **Fig. 17**

Let's look at a few more chromatic fragments which are common to a major sound—this time between the third and the fifth.

Fig. 18

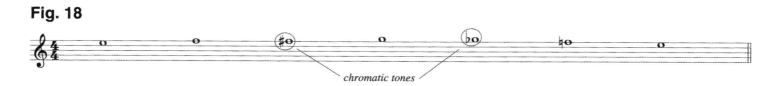

chromatic tones

See if you recognize this common sound…

Fig. 19

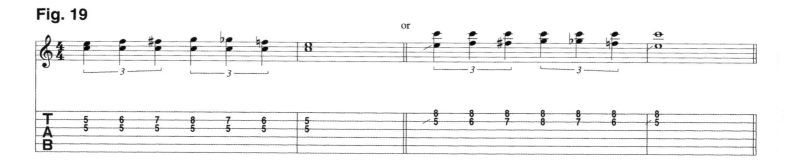

…or as single-note phrases similar to the following.

Fig. 20

THE BLUES SCALE

The C blues scale can sometimes be played on a C major scale with obviously bluesy results.

Fig. 21 - C Blues Scale

Another common use of the blues scale is to play it down a minor third from the root of the major chord you are soloing over. In other words, play the A blues scale over a C major sound.

Fig. 22 - A Blues Scale Over C

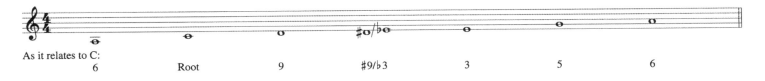

The chromatic note (sharp-two or flat-three) resolves in either direction.

Fig. 23

Here are a few typical bebop phrases that work over a major seventh sound.

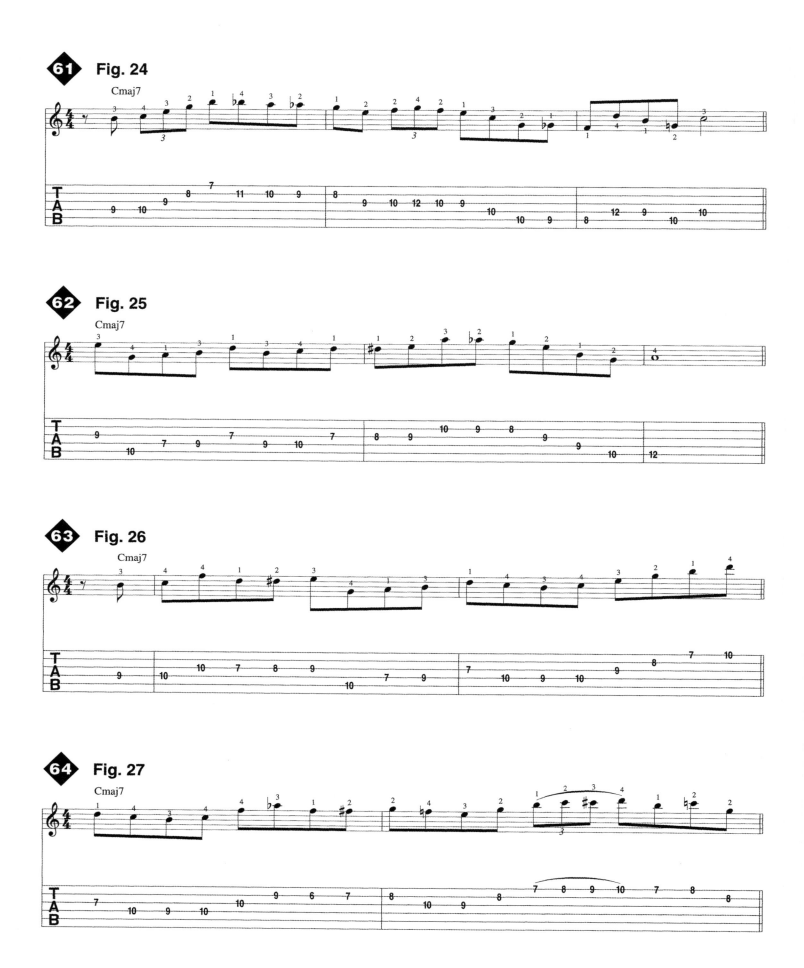

CHAPTER 7

NON-CHORD TONES

Suspensions, appoggiaturas, passing tones, and "surround" notes all fall into the category of non-chordal tones, or notes not part of the basic harmony. Playing only the chord tones, sometimes called "change running," simply reiterates the harmony already stated by the chordal instrument. In the beginning, we have to know the chord tones in order to make the changes. The next step is to build a vocabulary of melodic lines that implies the changes by embellishing the chord tones with passing tones or surround notes. Investigating transcriptions of (and transcribing) solos of great improvisers will reveal extensive use of chord tone embellishment.

This example from a Bach fugue displays the use of non-chord tones to create a beautiful melody.

65 **Fig. 1**

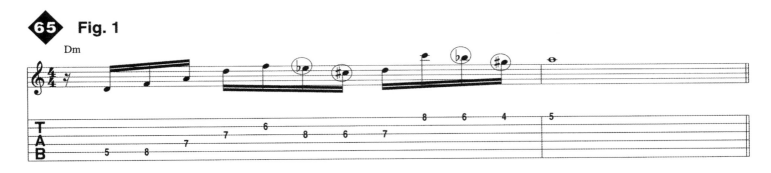

In the above example, the circled notes chromatically "surround" the root of the chord and the fifth.

In the next Charlie Parker-type phrase, the non-chord tones surround the fifth of D7 and approach the root from below.

66 **Fig. 2**

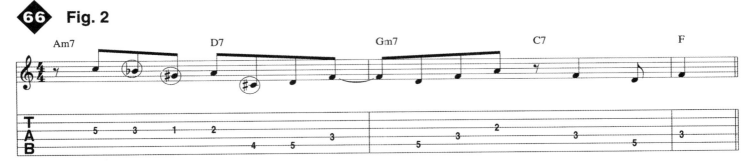

Here is a phrase in the style of Bird using non-chord tones to chromatically surround the third and the root.

67 **Fig. 3**

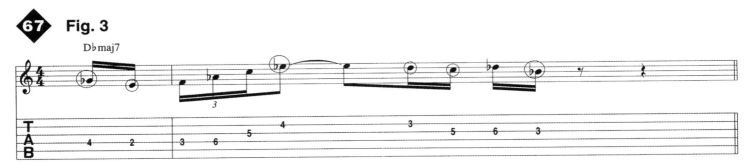

Here are some examples of passing tones and "surround" notes modelled after Charlie Parker.

68 **Fig. 4**

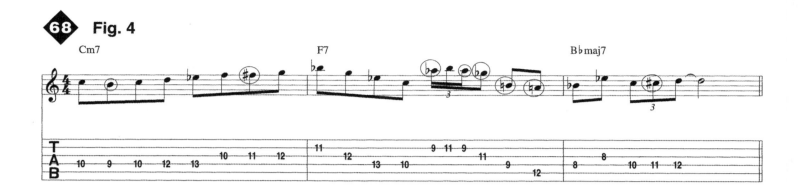

The following five lines highlight the use of non-chord tones.

69 **Fig. 5**

70 **Fig. 6**

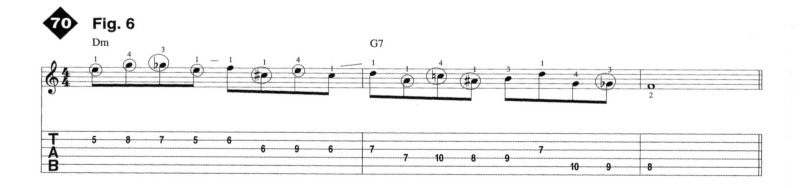

71 **Fig. 7**

72 **Fig. 8**

73 **Fig. 9**

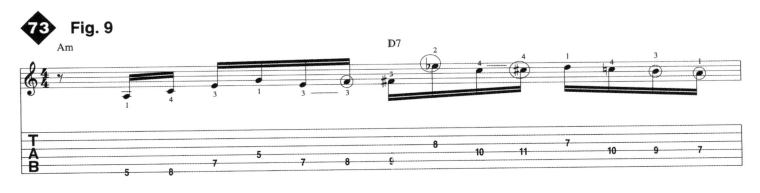

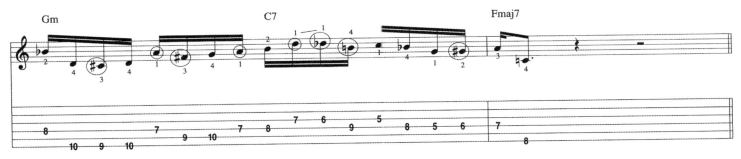

This long triplet line makes use of passing tones and surround notes.

74 **Fig. 10**

Here's more from the "cult of wrong notes." The following is a bebop-style phrase surrounding all the chord tones.

75 **Fig. 11**

There are no wrong notes.
—Miles Davis

There are actually no wrong notes. The way a musician deals with the tension created by non-chord tones is part of the improviser's art.

There are simple formulas for embellishing chord tones. One traditional way is by using notes a half step below the chord tone and a scale step (half or whole step) above.

Fig. 12A

Fig. 12B

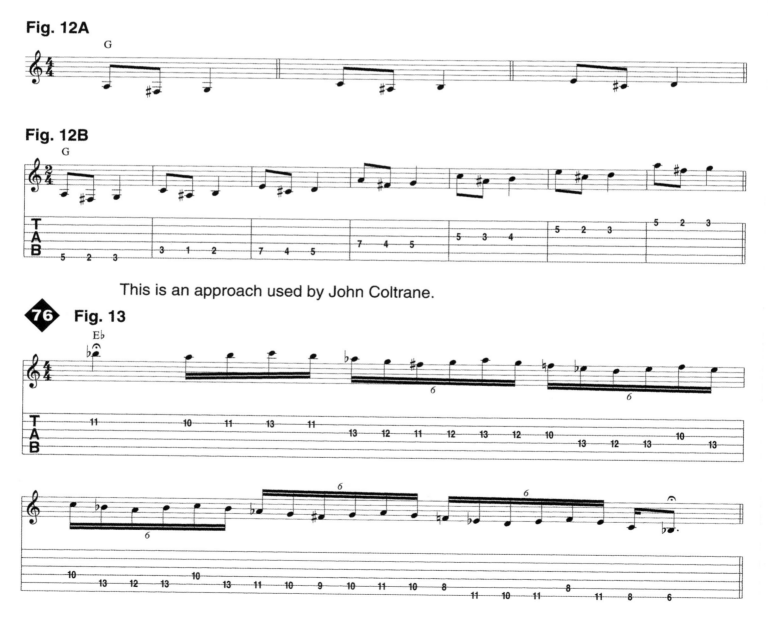

This is an approach used by John Coltrane.

76 **Fig. 13**

APPOGGIATURA CHORDS

An *appoggiatura* is a non-chordal tone on a stressed beat. If there are two or more appoggiaturas occurring simultaneously, the result is an *appoggiatura chord*.

This common substitution for E♭maj7 has been used in standard tunes, and is an example of appoggiatura.

77 ▶ Fig. 14

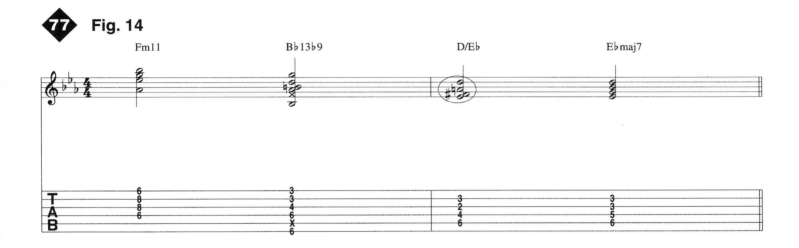

Here are several more examples of the way an appoggiatura chord has been used in standard tunes.

78 ▶ Fig. 15

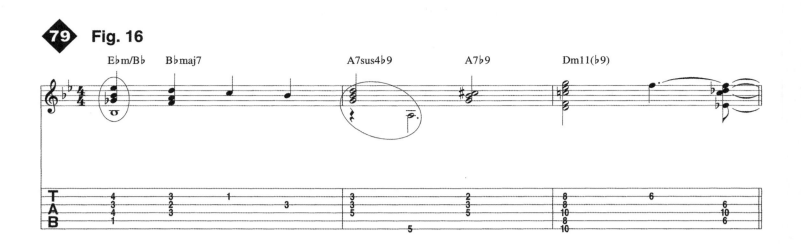

79 **Fig. 16**

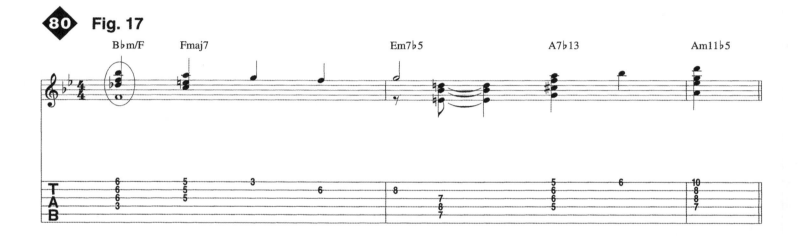

80 **Fig. 17**

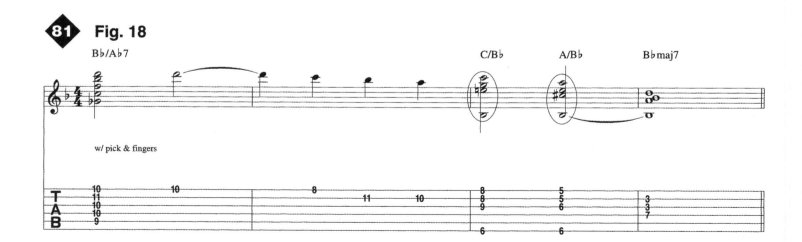

81 **Fig. 18**

PASSING CHORDS

Here are some examples of passing chords in chord solos.

 Fig. 19

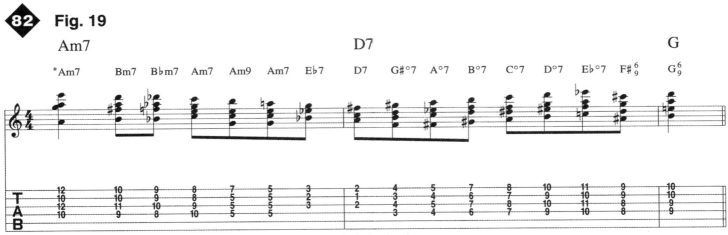

* Large chord symbols represent overall tonality; small chord symbols represent sub-chords and passing tones.

Fig. 20

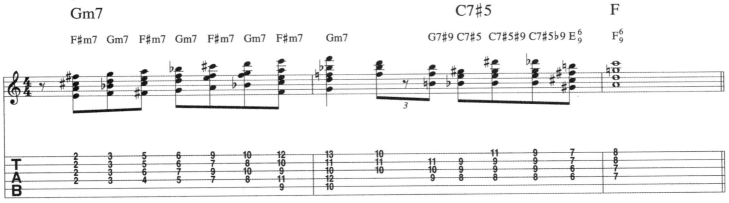

Fig. 21

83 A BLUES IN PASSING

by Sid Jacobs

CHAPTER 8

FOURTHS ▶

Fourths and the harmony derived from them is referred to as *quartal* harmony, in contrast to the traditional *tertial* harmony based on building chords in thirds. Quartal harmony has become an important aspect of contemporary harmony and jazz music of the post-bebop era.

Often when we encounter a 7sus4 chord in a piece of sheet music, the desired sound is a chord built on fourths or inversions of fourth chords. The nature of their sound is compatible with modal style playing and is used with a great deal of flexibility.

This next chord shape is quite commonly heard in modal situations. It is even colloquially referred to as the "So What" voicing because of its presence in Miles Davis's classic tune of the same name.

Fig. 1 - "So What" Chord

Combined with the same shape up a whole step, it has all the notes of the C major or D Dorian mode.

Fig. 2

Here's how it may be used in the context of a song.

Fig. 3

The following voicing works for Dm7 or Dm7sus4, but is also used for B♭6/9, E♭maj7(6/9), or A♭maj7♯11.

Fig. 4

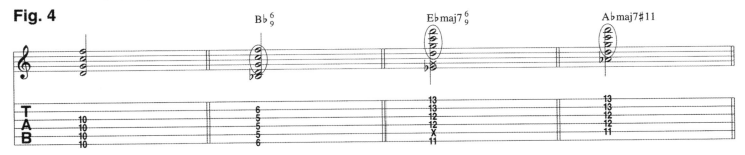

FOURTH CHORDS AND INVERSIONS

Practice these shapes in all keys in each inversion, and on all sets of strings: 1–2–3/2–3–4/3–4–5/4–5–6.

Fig. 5

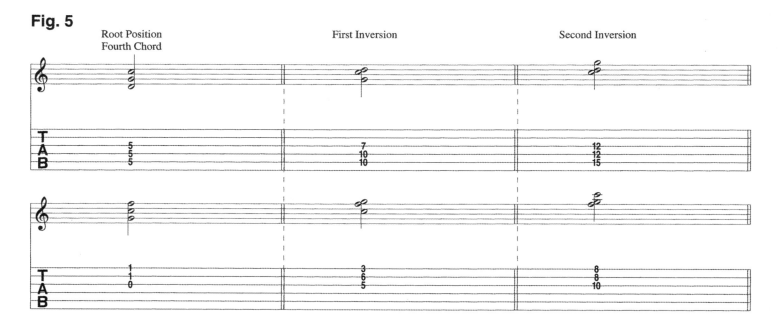

DIATONIC FOURTHS

Now let's build four-note fourth chord shapes from each scale tone in the C major scale.

84 Fig. 6

Since the melodic minor scale is identical to the major scale with the exception of the flatted-third degree, we can change the above example to melodic minor simply by changing the E natural to E♭.

84 (cont.) Fig. 7

The above fourth chords for C melodic minor will work well for F13♯11 and B7(alt.) situations. Try playing these chords over a low C, a low F, and B to hear and become accustomed to some of the uses of quartal harmony.

The next three figures build three-note fourth chords up the F major scale. Figure 8 is in root position, Figure 9 is in first inversion, and Figure 10 is in second inversion.

85 **Fig. 8 - Root Position F Major Fourth Chords**

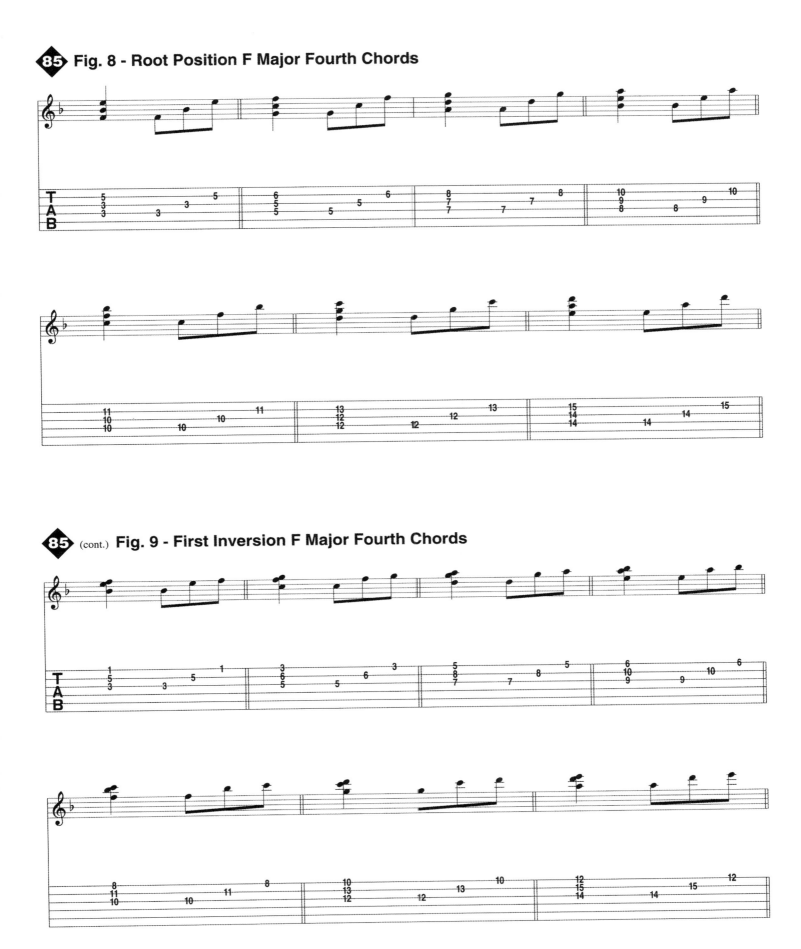

85 (cont.) **Fig. 9 - First Inversion F Major Fourth Chords**

The chord shapes built on the second, third, fifth, sixth, and seventh degrees are all identical, since they are all made up of perfect fourths. The inversions of these perfect fourth shapes will, naturally, also be the same.

85 (cont.) **Fig. 10 - Second Inversion F Major Fourth Chords**

To create lines using the previous chord shapes, one could play the shapes up the scale in triplets.

86 **Fig. 11**

Or, you could play Figure 11 as eighth notes.

86 (cont.) **Fig. 12**

You could also play the shapes forwards and backwards.

86 (cont.) **Fig. 13**

Try the above figure in eighth notes.

86 (cont.) **Fig. 14**

4THS MOVING IN 5THS LESSON ▶

Use your imagination to find more ways of turning these shapes into melodic ideas.

CHAPTER 9
FOURTHS CONTINUED

In this chapter we will build some fourth lines based on intervallic relationships. The next few examples take two notes a perfect fourth apart and transpose them in intervals of a tritone (a flatted fifth, sharped fourth, or six semitones), major thirds (four semitones), minor thirds (three semitones), and whole steps (two semitones). This is one technique of contemporary harmony we can use to create scales, melodic patterns, and find harmonies we wouldn't encounter from the diatonic scales. In these fourth lines we find the symmetrical scales, such as the diminished and augmented, that are such a big part of modern jazz.

FOURTHS STACKED IN A TRITONE

If we take a fourth interval and transpose it up a tritone, we get the following notes.

Fig. 1

As a melodic line, these notes create the tetratonic (tritone) scale.

Fig. 2 - Tetratonic Scale

The same notes occur when you play the previous line up a tritone.

Fig. 3

These four notes work well with the roots G and Db, and in either context suggest a 13#9 chord.

Fig. 4

	F	Bb/A#	B/Cb	E
G7	b7	#9	3	13
Db7	3	13	b7	#9

FOURTHS STACKED IN MAJOR THIRDS

In the next figure, we will take a perfect fourth interval and move it up in major thirds.

Fig. 5

As a melodic line, we get the following notes.

Fig. 6

The above fourth line yields the notes of the augmented scale. It will also yield the same notes (and harmony) if moved in major thirds in either direction.

Fig. 7 - Augmented Scale (for C, E, or Ab)

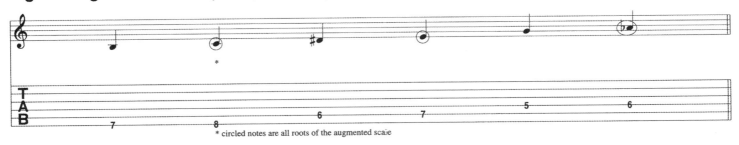

* circled notes are all roots of the augmented scale

Try this fourth idea over Cmaj7#5, Emaj7#5, or Amaj7#5. There is a lot of harmony in this scale—check it out.

FOURTHS STACKED IN MINOR THIRDS

The following figure transposes a perfect fourth up in minor thirds.

Fig. 8

As a melodic line, we get the following notes.

Fig. 9

 The above fourth line yields the same notes as the diminished scale.

Fig. 10 - Diminished Scale (for E♭, F♯, A, or C)

* circled notes are all roots of the diminished scale.

Try the above line over D7, F7, A♭7, and B7.

OBSERVATIONS ON FOURTHS

The whole tone scale in fourths yields all twelve notes.

87 **Fig. 11**

In this variation, the order of notes is altered.

87 (cont.) **Fig. 12**

Here is the same line descending.

87 (cont.) **Fig. 13**

Try the above line over anything!

Within the cycle of fourths, we have all twelve notes. After the first six notes in the cycle, we arrive at a note a tritone away from the starting note, beginning another group of six notes in fourths.

(C–F–B♭–E♭–A♭–D♭) (G♭–B–E–A–D–G)

A succession of five perfect fourths will yield the notes of the pentatonic scale.

E–A–D–G–C   FOURTHS
C–D–E–G–A   C MAJOR PENTATONIC

A succession of seven perfect fourths will yield the notes of the major scale.

B–E–A–D–G–C–F   FOURTHS
C–D–E–F–G–A–B   C MAJOR SCALE

And twelve successions of perfect fourths will yield all the notes of the chromatic scale.

C–F–B♭–E♭–A♭–D♭–G♭–B–E–A–D–G

C–D♭–D–E♭–E–F–G♭–G–A♭–A–B♭–B

If we break this twelve note cycle into groups of three, we see a minor third progression.

(C–F–B♭–) (E♭–A♭–D♭) (G♭–B–E) (A–D–G)

If we break this cycle into groups of four, we see a progression of descending major thirds.

(C–F–B♭–E♭) (A♭–D♭–G♭–B) (E–A–D–G)

FOUR-NOTE CHORD SHAPES IN 4THS LESSON

4THS MOVING IN MAJOR 2NDS LESSON

Another way to obtain all twelve tones with fourths is by moving a three-note grouping of perfect fourths up in minor thirds.

Fig. 14

A four-note group moved down in major thirds is yet another way to get all twelve tones.

Fig. 15

Here is a phrase based on the previous figure.

88 Fig. 16

These two lines use four-note phrases moved up a minor sixth or down a minor third (in these examples, up a fourth=down a fifth).

Another observation: After five successive perfect fourths, we arrive at a pitch a semitone away.

C–F–B♭–E♭–A♭–D♭

This line takes a five-note fourth shape and moves it up chromatically.

And finally, one more twelve-note line.

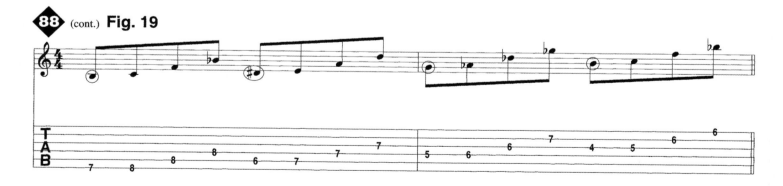

4THS AND THE AUGMENTED TRIAD LESSON

CHAPTER 10

MORE FOURTHS AND FIFTHS

In experimenting with fourths and fifths, we can take a melodic shape and sequence it through the scale. All these work in the C major tonality and corresponding modes. This phrase is in the style of Joe Diorio. The circled notes are an ascending C major scale.

89 **Fig. 1**

As with all examples, transpose the above figure to all keys. These shapes also sound good backward or forward-and-backward.

90 **Fig. 2**

Try this line over harmonies from the G major tonality, such as Am7, D7, and Cmaj7♭5.

91 **Fig. 3**

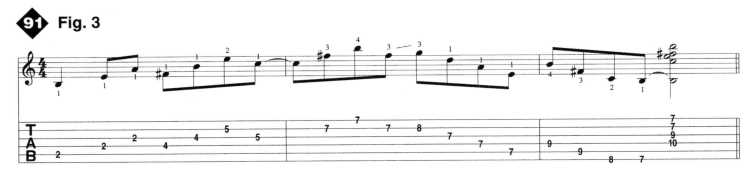

Try the next two over a Cm7 or an F7 sound.

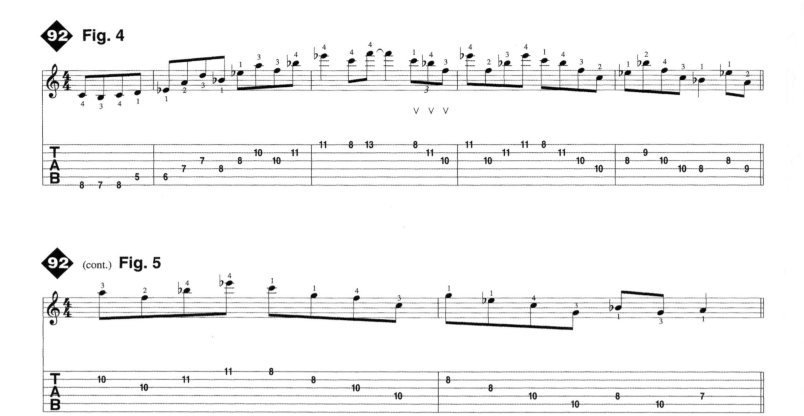

92 Fig. 4

92 (cont.) Fig. 5

These two lines work well with fourth chords in the key of D and related modes.

93 Fig. 6

93 (cont.) Fig. 7

Try this line with fourth chords from the key of C and related modes.

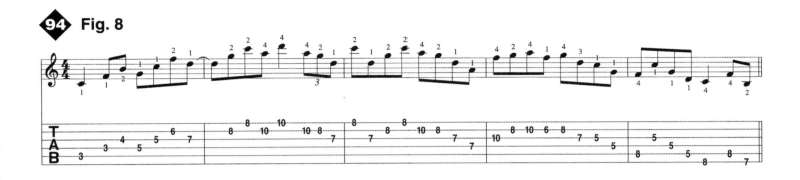

This one works over Gm.

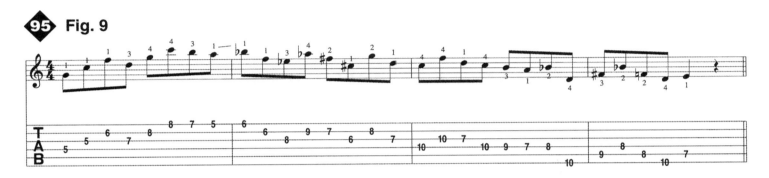

Try these two over Fmaj7♭5 or G13.

This one works well over Fm or B♭7.

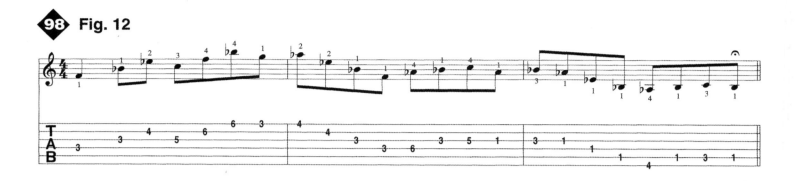

98 **Fig. 12**

We'll finish with a complete piece. This etude uses fourth lines and is based on a blues progression.

99 # FOURTH DEMENTIA

by Sid Jacobs